MN00709548

ANIMALS

ANIMALS

Louise Miller

VGM Career Horizons
a division of *NTC Publishing Group*
Lincolnwood, Illinois USA

Photo Credits:
Page 1: Philadelphia Zoo; pages 15, 29, and 43:
Photo Network; pages 57 and 65: Trisha Miller
Communications; page 71: United States Bureau
of Sport Fisheries & Wildlife/Jack F. Dermid.

All other photographs courtesy of the authors.

Miller, Louise
    Career Portraits. Animals/Louise Miller.
      p.   cm.
    ISBN 0–8442–4359–0
    1. Animal specialists—Vocational guidance—Juvenile literature. 2. Animal
specialists—Biography—Juvenile literature. [1. Animal specialists—Vocational
guidance. 2. Vocational guidance. 3. Occupations.] I. Title.
SF80.M54 1995
636'.0023—dc20   93–49056
                                                    CIP
                                                      AC

Published by VGM Career Horizons, a division of NTC Publishing Group
4255 West Touhy Avenue
Lincolnwood (Chicago), Illinois 60646-1975, U.S.A.
© 1995 by NTC Publishing Group. All rights reserved.
No part of this book may be reproduced, stored in a retrieval system,
or transmitted in any form or by any means,
electronic, mechanical, photocopying, recording or otherwise,
without the prior permission of NTC Publishing Group.
Manufactured in the United States of America.

7 8 9 ML 9 8 7 6 5 4 3 2

Contents

I never saw a Purple Cow,
I never hope to see one;
But I can tell you, anyhow,
I'd rather see than be one.

Gelett Burgess, 1866–1951

Introduction

A privilege, an honor, a pleasure—these words describe
what people think about "their" animals. The animals are
the reasons they get up in the morning and provide their
main job satisfaction throughout the sometimes long and
tiring days. People who work with animals love them.
And they love the diversity of the choices they have in
their work.

When you choose a career with animals, you have a lot
of options. You may choose to become a veterinarian and
take care of sick and injured animals. Or you may choose
to assist the veterinarian with all the responsibilities surrounding the animals' care.

You may want to help other people understand animal
behavior and needs. You can choose whether you want to
work with dogs, cats, horses, elephants, giraffes, tigers,
lions, cows, chickens, snakes, or birds. You can work in a
zoo, in an aquarium, in a stable, on a farm, at a race track,
or in an animal shelter. You can open up your own shop
or work for someone else. You can work full time or part
time. You can work for the government or for a private
corporation.

For some jobs, you will need a great deal of education,
training, and skills. For others, you will receive on-the-job
training. You alone can make the choice that best suits you.
So let's start exploring the wonderful world of animals!

CAREERS

IN

ZOOS

All of us have been to the zoo at one time or another. We love to see animals that we cannot ordinarily see in the city or on the farm. Where else can we see an elephant, a giraffe, or a tiger? We don't find antelopes, apes, or lions in our backyards. Going to the zoo is a great family outing because we learn so much from the animals and begin to understand their needs. That is precisely the point of the modern zoo—to teach humans about the various species that we share our planet with. Another function of today's zoo is to breed animals in a habitat much like their original one in order to preserve the species.

1

What it's like to be a zoo employee

More than 120 million people visit zoos every year in North America. And there are about 11,000 full-time employees in those zoos. That means that there are many jobs that are possible to think about for careers.

These jobs include: director, assistant director, curator, scientist, zookeeper, zoologist, and veterinarian. Zoos also need gardeners, veterinary technicians, business managers, operations managers, public relations specialists, and a clerical staff. Many zoos also have a library and an educational department.

If you want to work directly with the animals, as a zookeeper does, you will need a college degree, preferably in biology or zoology. Managers may need an advanced degree in an animal science or business curriculum. You may also have to take an examination before you are hired.

Let's find out what happens on the job

The director has the top position in the zoo. If you were the director, you would be responsible for the smooth running of the zoo on a daily basis and for any future growth and development.

A general curator sees to the whole animal collection; there may be various curators for specific departments, such as mammals, birds, research, or education.

Veterinarians and veterinary technicians take care of the general health and well-being of all the animals in the zoo. Zoologists are in charge of developing the various collections for the zoo.

The zookeepers take care of the animals on a daily basis; they clean and maintain the animals' habitats and make sure they get fed the proper food. If there is any change in the animals' behavior, the zoo-keeper will probably be the first one to notice it.

The pleasures and pressures of the job

The main pleasure of any job that has to do with animals is working directly with them, no matter how difficult or strenuous the work may be. When you are a manager, your chief job will be to see to it that the animals are being well taken care of. The pressures come in when the animal is sick or injured, when an emergency occurs, or when there is not enough staff to take proper care of the animals.

Some people who work in zoos also feel that being part of preserving endangered species is one of the major pleasures of this job. Still others feel that educating the public about the various species and their needs and behavioral patterns would rank high in their list of pleasures.

The rewards, the pay, and the perks

The privilege of working with animals seems to be more important than anything else to the people who do it. And that's good, because you may never make a lot of money if you work in a zoo. Each zoo will have a different pay scale, depending on its size and budget and the educational and training requirements necessary for the job. But even with a college degree, your starting salary will probably be lower than you might have wanted. Zoos, like aquariums, usually have good insurance plans, opportunities for advancement, and a fairly good vacation policy. So if you really love animals and would be able to live on a budget, your future may be in a zoo.

Getting started

Generally speaking, if you want to work directly with the animals or want to move up the ladder to management, you will have to have a college degree. As a zookeeper, zoologist, or veterinarian, it is required in most places. Even if you should get a job as a zookeeper with only a high school diploma, you would generally not be able to be promoted beyond that level. If you plan to go on to middle or top management positions, a master's degree or even a Ph.D. may be required.

In high school, be sure that your grades are very good in science, math, and English. Computer skills will also be important. Any volunteer work at a veterinarian's office, in a zoo, or in a pet store can be very helpful. If you have a family pet, think about how responsible you have been in its care and feeding. Many television shows are now showing wild animal behavioral patterns and needs. Think about watching them instead of cartoons, sitcoms, or MTV. The sooner you start thinking about your future, the better.

Climbing the career ladder

Most people will start out as a zookeeper. After a few years, you may become a senior zookeeper. From there you may become an assistant curator and then curator of a particular department, such as mammals or birds. Then you may become a general curator. From there, you may become the assistant director and then director.

Since most zoos are large institutions, often run like a business, managers have to have highly developed communication and business skills, in addition to a solid working knowledge of the animals in the collection. Since most zoos are not-for-profit organizations, a director has to be a goodwill ambassador and fund-raiser.

Let's Meet...

Bonnie Jacobs
Senior Zookeeper

Bonnie has been a keeper at a major zoo in a large city for 12 years. She is now a senior keeper in the primate house. She says it is a privilege to work with endangered species every day.

Tell me how you got started in zoo work.

I got my start by answering an ad in the newspaper for a three-month internship at a major zoo. After this internship, I applied for zookeeper jobs there and at another local zoo. My original dream was to do field work in Africa like Jane Goodall, but maybe working in the primate house of a major zoo in the United States isn't too far from that dream after all.

Describe a typical day at work.

I arrive at work at 7:45 in the morning and change into work clothes. The first thing I do is "damage control"—I check the animals' health and behavior and all their habitats. Then I remove the animals from the exhibits to feed them. After that, I clean all the exhibits and add any additional items to their diet as necessary. All the animals are back on exhibit and ready for the public by 10 A.M.

Then all the areas in back have to be cleaned. Then I have to prepare the food for the next day. By 5 P.M. when the zoo closes, all the animals have to be brought in for the night.

What schooling or training did you need to get this job?

This zoo is run by the municipal park district, which requires only a high school diploma to become a zookeeper. Most other zoos do require a college degree, preferably in biology or a related field. I have a bachelor's degree in psychology with an emphasis on animal behavior. I also did some research at a primate laboratory, but most of my training was on the job.

What do you like most/least about your job?

My greatest pleasure is the privilege of working with endangered animals on a daily basis. The part I like least is seeing animals become sick. The worst part is, of course, when an animal dies. This is particularly difficult when the animals have been there a while and I have worked closely with them.

What advice do you have for young people who are interested in zookeeping?

Good communication skills are important. A background in biology and research skills help. A zookeeper also has to be physically fit to do the job well, because there is a lot of physical work with large animals. You have to think quickly as a zookeeper; you should start acquiring these skills at a young age. Volunteer at your local zoo or get a job with a veterinarian.

High Points in Bonnie's Career

One of Bonnie's most vivid memories of her first day on the job as an intern was of cockroaches. Since she had never seen one before, she was appalled. She had nightmares about them for weeks!

When she got her job as senior zookeeper, she was ecstatic. She also felt confident because she had the skills to perform the job. Because of her skills and experience, she knew she deserved the promotion.

Bonnie says her work environment is challenging, fun, and exciting. She also says it is hard physical work. Bonnie says one of the most difficult parts of her job is sorting out problems among the various personnel.

Teamwork is important on this job since there are only four people working in her building. Each one is important to get the job done.

The most memorable moments for Bonnie are the births that she has seen over the years—and she has seen many. However, she says that one of her happiest moments was when she got the promotion to senior keeper in the new primate house. She was in the reptile house at the time, but her primary interest was primates and she had been hoping at least to move there. It was wonderful to move there as a senior keeper!

Let's Meet...

Kevin Bell
Zoo Director

Kevin Bell practically grew up in a zoo. His father was a zookeeper in New York and the family lived on the zoo grounds.

Describe a typical day at work.

Now that I am in management, my typical days often consist of one meeting after another. Generally they start at 8 A.M. These meetings usually have to do with three major areas of modern zoos: finance, conservation, and education. We discuss these areas both in the short term and in the long term. Decisions have to be made on a daily basis for the everyday problems, but the director of the zoo has to plan for the future in these three areas, too. Since many zoos are not-for-profit organizations, fund-raising becomes very important for the director. Much of this money goes for the care of the existing animals and for the conservation of the species. Educating the public to the needs of wild animals is the third major area of concern.

What schooling or training did you need to get this job?

I have a bachelor's degree in biology and a master's degree in zoology. But I also bring management skills to the job, especially those having to do with managing personnel. My major background in zoos was with birds and mammals. I designed the bird house and in a way hated to leave it for an administrative position. But I have a very capable staff that I know very well because of my many years' experience in this zoo. Together we plan to make the zoo a better place in the future for the birds, animals, and visitors.

What do you like most/least about your job?

I like interacting with people most, and that means at all levels. When it was announced that I was to be the new director, the whole community seemed to greet me with enthusiasm. Everything so far seems to suit me well because of my long experience with zoos and my ability to meet this new challenge.

Although I spent two years as a curator before I accepted the position of director, I do miss working with the animals—especially the birds, my first love. I also feel I have lost control of my daily routine because everything is scheduled for me now. Meetings are scheduled weeks in advance and I really do not have much say in the who, what, when, and where of my day. I do thank my lucky stars for my secretary, who takes such able control of my day.

How Kevin's Job Rewards Him

Kevin says his most unforgettable experience on the job was releasing birds back into the wild. He first experienced it as a child, but thinks it is still a thrill today—and the real point of breeding various species in captivity.

Kevin didn't get into zoo work or aspire to management for the money. He says his father told him early on that the zoo was no place to become a millionaire. The rewards of the job are in seeing to it that the animals are well taken care of and in working with members of the community to plan for the future of the zoo.

Although Kevin admits to being somewhat of a loner, he thinks of himself as a good team player, because he has to work with staff members, departments heads, city leaders, and park district personnel to make the zoo function smoothly.

His days are full and sometimes he does not have time to get everything done. He brings work home with him. He has an office in the administration building and not in the middle of the bird house as he did before. He has to plan renovation projects, develop educational projects, and attend meetings all day long. Would he change it? Never! Kevin has reached his ultimate goal and is flying high.

Success Stories

Jack Hanna   Jack Hanna, lively director of the Colum-
bus, Ohio, Zoo since 1978, is someone you
may already know. He has appeared with a
wide and wild variety of zoo animals on
such television shows as "Good Morning
America" and "Larry King Live." He now has his own TV
show, "ZooLife with Jack Hanna." He also has written a
book, *Monkeys on the Interstate.* Along with his love of
animals, he believes in entertaining people while teaching
them about wild animals.

Jack has traveled to India, Europe, Africa, South
America, the Galapagos Islands, and China in the past five
years.

The San Diego Zoo   The world-famous San Diego
Zoo, now 77 years old, has
4,000 animals of 800 species
housed in barless, moated
habitats that resemble their
homes in the wild. The zoo contains a children's zoo, a
botanical garden with 6,500 plant species, the Center of
Reproduction of Endangered Species, an Asian rain forest, a
sun bear forest, and a gorilla tropics area. You can see all
this on land with the bus tour or from 170 feet above it all in
the Skyfari.

Find Out More

You and the zoo

After reading about these two possible career opportunities, you should have formed some ideas about whether you might be interested in zoo work. Let's take a look at some of the skills and training you'll need for these jobs.

Zookeeper
- Physical strength and fitness
- Knowledge of animals' needs
- Good communication skills
- College degree, preferably in biology or zoology
- Ability to make quick decisions

Zoo manager
- Experience as a keeper or assistant director
- Good communication, computer, and business skills
- Fund-raising skills
- College degree, preferably a master's degree
- Ability to get along with other people

Can you come up with five good reasons to become a zookeeper?

Now come up with five reasons to become a zoo manager.

At this point, you should have a pretty good idea about whether zoo life is for you, so don't cage yourself in. Follow that wild idea, and feel free to choose just what you would do best in the zoo.

To find out more about zoos, contact:

The American Association of Zoo Keepers
Topeka Zoological Park
635 S. W. Gage Blvd.
Topeka, KS 66606-2066

Zoo Jobs
Office of Education-Information
National Zoological Park
Washington, DC 20009

Zoo and Aquarium Careers
The American Association of Zoological Parks and Aquariums
Oglebay Park
Wheeling, WV 26003

CAREERS IN VETERINARY WORK

B ecoming a veterinarian requires a lot of time and a lot of study. After all, they are doctors and they have a great deal to learn about all kinds of animals. In that sense, it is more difficult than being a doctor for humans.

But once you are a veterinarian, you have quite a few career possibilities. You may go into private practice or work at a zoo, aquarium, shelter, or farm, depending on which type of animal you want to work with.

Very often you will be working with a veterinary technician. These technicians help veterinarians by recording
patient information, preparing patients for surgery, and
performing specific laboratory work. Technicians may also
double as animal care attendants, depending on the size of
the facility. They always work under the supervision of the
veterinarian or senior attendant.

What it's like to be in veterinary work

Both veterinarians and veterinary
technicians work directly with the
animals and each other. But the
duties and educational requirements of each are quite different.

Both are responsible for the
health and well-being of the animals in their care; those animals
can range from cats and dogs, cows
and pigs, or sparrows and parrots to
gorillas and giraffes. Even dogs and
cats require constant care when
they are sick, injured, or recovering
from surgery. So if you are thinking
about veterinary work, be prepared
to use your brawn as well as your
brain.

Let's find out what happens on the job

Most people who become veterinarians will work in private practice, in
an animal hospital. They will be
working mainly with pets, such as
dogs and cats. Others specialize in
wild or farm animals, birds, or
horses. All told, veterinarians take
care of millions of animals a year.
Veterinarians can also become

researchers or teachers, or they can work as inspectors for state or federal agencies. Some even work as animal control workers or for the environment. Still others work to keep diseases in livestock from becoming public health hazards.

As a veterinarian, you could also work in pharmacology, microbiology, or quality control for major corporations. Even though there are many possibilities for places to work, all veterinarians and veterinary technicians must respect animals and want to see that they are well taken care of.

The pleasures and pressures of the job

The main pleasure of veterinary work is seeing sick or injured animals recover, seeing the happiness of the owners when their pet is going home after surgery, and knowing that you have contributed to this health and happiness.

Of course, people who have to make life-and-death decisions, perform operations, and sometimes bring bad news to owners experience stress every day.

The veterinary technician also experiences physical stress because of the often physically strenuous work of picking up and moving animals, lifting cartons of food and litter, and cleaning up rooms and kennels. None of it is easy, but it is rewarding to see a wagging tail and feel a wet nose on your cheek!

The rewards, the pay, and the perks

Most people who work with animals will tell you that they do not do it for the money. This is not to say that you cannot live comfortably as a veterinarian or a veterinary technician, but money will probably not be on the top of the list of rewards. Salaries will vary from place to place, from city to farm, from zoo to aquarium. Corporations may pay more than small private practices; jobs in big cities usually pay more than those in small towns.

Many veterinarians count the variety of opportunity and the fact that the employment outlook is so good as important perks of the job. More and more people have pets and these owners seem to realize how important preventive medicine and good medical care are. There are also very good possibilities for specialists, such as orthopedists, surgeons, ophthalmologists, cardiologists, and dermatologists. Some veterinarians are also specializing in animal behavior.

Getting started

Usually you will not find jobs for veterinarians advertised in the local newspaper. Most graduates of veterinary schools have to count on professional journals that advertise available positions or networking with other professionals.

Veterinary technicians may be able to get started as volunteers at an animal hospital, zoo, shelter, or aquarium, and then apply to them directly. You may start out as a kennel or animal care attendant. Later you can learn the specific responsibilities of the technician.

Climbing the career ladder

Veterinarians have to take a national qualifying exam in order to practice, and they also have to be licensed or certified in the state where they will be working. Licenses and certificates usually have to be renewed every year. They also have to continue their education by attending meetings sponsored by the American Veterinary Medical Association.

Now decide if veterinary work is right for you

If you decide to become a veterinarian, you will have to be prepared for years of schooling. In addition to 4 years in college, you will have to attend an additional 3 years at a veterinary college. There are fewer than 30 accredited veterinary schools in the United States, so the competition to get accepted is very intense.

Let's Meet...

Kathleen Deering
Veterinarian

Kathleen works in an animal hospital in a large city. She is very pleased with the work that she does and looks forward to a lifetime of working with animals.

Tell me how you got started in veterinary work.

I was always sure that I wanted to be a veterinarian. I always had pets and maybe that was because of my father's love of animals. I got my bachelor's degree in biology and my master's in molecular biology. I started applying for veterinarian school late in my college career and was not accepted until my third try.

What schooling or training did you need to get this job?

I had a broad-based education in college and graduated with a B.S. in biology, a very good degree to have if you plan to become a veterinarian. Since there are so few veterinary schools, check with them first to see what their requirements may be. Then you can plan your college courses with graduate school requirements in mind. You should plan on studying science, English, and computer skills if possible.

What do you like most/least about your job?

I like the variety of work in an animal hospital. A veterinarian has to be prepared to work not only with the animals, but also with the owners, who are usually under stress. I do not like cruelty to or neglect of the animals. I am also always stressed when owners are looking for a "quick fix" for the sick animal. Sometimes owners forget that animals have complex bodies that might need X-rays, blood work, or some other laboratory workup that will take some time for analysis and diagnosis. I have to work with people more than I thought I would, and that is not always easy or predictable.

What advice do you have for young people interested in veterinary work?

Enjoy animals, take care of animals, and be responsible.

Pet-sitting is very popular today because more and more people have pets and many of them are at work all day. As soon as you are old enough, volunteer at any organization that will allow you to work directly with animals.

Kathleen's Typical Workday

Kathleen starts out every morning by checking all the sick animals. She then looks over all the animals that had surgery on the previous day. Those that are ready to go home are cleaned up. From about 10 A.M. to 12 P.M. she performs surgery and then has a two-hour lunch period, if she is lucky. Sometimes, depending on the work load, she will work through lunch. Surgeries can be fairly routine, such as spaying or neutering, although dental work is becoming very popular. Afternoons are devoted to seeing clients, taking X-rays, and preparing animals for the next day's surgeries. Usually there are 5 to 15 sick animals in the hospital at any one time. When the surgery is over, it is particularly important to watch those animals' progress.

Let's Meet...

Carol Nishioka
Veterinary Technician

Carol works closely with the veterinarians at an animal hospital. She has been there for 7 years and hopes to be working with animals for the rest of her life.

Describe a typical day at work.

In the morning, I give treatments to the animals, check on the previous day's surgeries, give shots, clean the cages, and feed the animals. Then I walk the dogs. I start at 8 A.M. and clients start coming in at 9 A.M. That is when I begin to assist the veterinarians with the new patients. I do that, and anything else that has to be done, until quitting time. As I make my rounds and clean the cages, I let the veterinarian know whether any animal needs particular attention.

What schooling or training did you need to get this job?

I have my high school equivalency diploma. I think that you should get at least a high school diploma if you are thinking about becoming a veterinary technician. I got all my training on the job, but I do recommend taking science, math, biology, and computer courses in high

school. Some hospitals may even require a
college degree, so you should check that out
with your counselor in high school. It is also
very important to follow instructions for
this job.

What do you like most/least about your job?

I like the dress code the best. Who wouldn't
like to wear jeans and gym shoes to work?
I like the comfortable clothes, the relaxed
atmosphere, and not wearing makeup. I also
love to see an animal recover from a disease,
injury, or surgery. I think my pay is quite
adequate.

I don't like the long hours. I work from
8 A.M. to 7 P.M. or later. Sometimes I am lucky
to get lunch. I am always on my feet and the
work is physically strenuous. Because of so
much lifting, hauling, pushing, and pulling,
I am full of aches and pains and am developing carpal tunnel syndrome. I always think
about the animals, even when I am home.

What advice do you have for young people interested in working as a veterinary technician?

Have a pet and take responsibility for it. I
have eight cats, and they are all indoor cats.
Get a summer job as a kennel worker as soon
as you are old enough or at least work as a
volunteer in order to get experience. You
should also learn to be strong enough to be
able to let an animal go when it is ready to die.

How Carol Got Her Job

Carol has always liked animals, but she never thought she could be a veterinarian. She really did not know what she wanted to do after high school so she tried a variety of jobs that she did not like. Then she asked herself what she really wanted to do. Her answer: Work with animals.

At that point, she got out the phone book and called every veterinarian and shelter in the city. Every one of them asked for previous experience. She finally got to the end of the alphabet, where she found the hospital she has been working at for 7 years. Two people were leaving at that time and she was hired as an animal attendant. Since she had no training, she received it all there.

After finally getting her first job with animals, Carol was terrified that her new employers would find out she was allergic to cats! She was sure they would fire her, so she kept taking allergy pills so they would not catch on. Even though she would occasionally sneeze, everyone seemed to think that she had a perpetual cold. Her allergy has gotten better and she has been there for 7 years.

Success Stories

Donna Alexander

Donna Alexander, chief veterinarian of a major animal care and control center in a large city, has quite a story to tell. She did not grow up on a farm; she grew up in an urban ghetto. But she knew when she was only 7 that she wanted to be a veterinarian. Her path was not easy, though. In high school her counselor did not seem to understand what it took to become a veterinarian, so her 4 years in college and the fierce competition to get into a veterinary school presented big challenges to this young but persistent woman.

Even in high school, Dr. Alexander showed a will to overcome hardships. She graduated first in her class, was a member of the National Honor Society, and was a Presidential Scholar. She could have become a top model, but she wanted to be a veterinarian.

She got her bachelor's degree from the University of Pennsylvania in microbiology and applied for veterinary school. Her excellent scholastic record and her volunteer work at the zoo and with veterinarians made her one of very few who were accepted.

Although she does not regret her decision for a moment, Dr. Alexander admits that it is not a glamorous job. She puts in long and strenuous hours. But she believes that compassion and a sense of humor, along with a firm scientific background, will get you through a lifetime of challenges.

James Herriot, well-known veterinarian and writer, was born in Scotland but did most of his work in his beloved Yorkshire, England. Herriot is a prolific writer of books about his life. You may have read one of them: *All Things Bright & Beautiful, All Things Wise and Wonderful, All Creatures Great & Small,* and *The Lord God Made Them All* are among his most popular. There is also a television show about his life and work that you may have seen.

These books are among the best about the everyday life of a country veterinarian with all the drama and simplicity that such a life entails. They are real stories about real people and animals and their lives. Herriot is not only a role model for all veterinarians, but also one of the most popular writers in the world today. You will be inspired by reading any of these wonderful books.

Find Out More

You and veterinary work

If you think that veterinary work might be just the thing for you, think of five characteristics or qualities of yours that are suitable to this work and give examples of things you have done to demonstrate these qualities. Now think about any times you have had to take responsibility for an animal and explain how you took care of it. If you have never had any experience with animals, talk about what you would do to take care of a cat or dog on an everyday basis or when the animal is sick.

Find out more about veterinary work

American Veterinary Medical
   Association
930 N. Meacham Road
Schaumburg, IL 60196

"Veterinarians" (Occupational
   Brief 83)
Chronicle Guidance Publications
Aurora Street Extension
P.O. Box 1190
Moravia, NY

"Veterinary Technicians" (Occupational Brief 480)
Chronicle Guidance Publications,
Aurora Street Extension
P.O. Box 1190
Moravia, NY 13118–1190

CAREERS IN HUMANE SHELTERS

An animal shelter is set up to take in animals on a temporary basis for rehabilitation and eventual adoption. In a large animal shelter in a big city, as many as 20,000 animals may be brought to the door in the course of a year. You will find many people performing various jobs at a shelter, including veterinarians, veterinary technicians, animal care attendants, managers, receptionists, and secretaries. Most shelters also rely on the work of many volunteers to keep things going.

The most important quality for any one of the workers is, of course, a love of animals and a deep commitment to their well-being. Knowing that stray, sick, or injured animals will be taken care of can be your most important reward if you choose to do humane work.

What it's like to work in a humane shelter

One of the primary functions of today's humane shelter is to provide information to the public on how to be responsible owners of pets and to eventually eliminate the need for shelters. For if we all truly cared about animals and followed the rules about neutering and spaying them, gave them routine medical care and nutrition, and were not cruel to them, there would hardly be a need for shelters. Our own homes would be places of shelter for the animals.

The pleasures and pressures of the job

One of the main purposes of humane education is to prevent cruelty, abuse, and harm to animals. When humane workers see so many abandoned and abused animals, they have to count that as the No. 1 pressure of the job. Also, the policy at many shelters is that an animal must be put to sleep if it isn't adopted after a certain period of time. That can be particularly stressful, especially when the animal is young and healthy. Dealing with people who may be turned down for adoption is also a stressful situation.

On the other hand, knowing that you might have prevented some cruelty or abuse of any animal through your educational programs is a great pleasure for a humane educator. Realizing that a new generation of people and animals may live in harmony is a big reward.

The rewards, the pay, and the perks

There are many rewards to humane work, but if you want to make a lot of money, this is not the job for you. Obviously the pay range will vary from shelter to shelter and city to city, and it will be adequate to live on. Many shelters do have a rather generous insurance program and will provide part, if not all, of your tuition money if you want to continue your education.

One of the best things about working in a shelter is seeing that animals find good homes and that they are healthy and happy there. Teaching children about humane treatment of animals and answering questions that worried owners have about their puppies and kitties is also very rewarding.

Getting started

There is no one typical educational path to working in humane shelters, but there might be some guidelines you can follow. You should know about animals. This does not necessarily mean that you have to be a biology major in college, but some basic courses in the sciences, math, English, animal behavior, psychology, and education would help. Working with animals in a shelter, zoo, or aquarium will give you the kind of hands-on experience that might convince an employer that you are serious about your work.

Since you may be called on to produce newsletters, pamphlets, or brochures, you may even want to take some journalism courses in high school or college. Or you might want to work on the yearbook or school newspaper. Computer skills are also very important for creating these materials and data bases. Any work in graphic design could help you in putting together exciting educational handouts.

On top of all that, you should have good research and public speaking skills, as well as a working knowledge of setting up a library according to title, author, and topic. This requires a high level of organizational abilities.

Climbing the career ladder

One way to start out with a humane shelter is as a humane educator, the one who actually goes out to the schools and libraries to spread the word about humane treatment and care of animals. The next move up would be to executive director of development, which means that you would be raising funds for the shelter. From there, you would advance to director of operations and then possibly to director of the shelter. Depending on the shelter, you could need a degree from a four-year college to be the manager of the education department, and, perhaps, a master's degree to advance any higher.

Things you can do to get a head start

Your education is a very important part of preparing for a career in humane shelters. A general curriculum in high school will suffice, but during that time you may want to do volunteer work in a shelter, work on the school newspaper, or be a member of the debating club, theater group, or speech club.

In college, you should get a broad-based liberal arts background in your first two years including science, speech, composition, math, and education courses. Keep up with outside activities or any part-time or vacation work with animals.

Let's Meet...

John Caruso
Humane Education Manager

John Caruso started out as a humane educator and worked his way up to manager. He is a creative, enthusiastic person who has a real commitment to young people, animals, and education.

Tell me how you got started in humane education.

I started out by applying for a job in the customer service department at the shelter, but because of my education, I became a humane educator.

I am sure that my background in public speaking and theater helped me become a good educator. You really cannot be afraid to stand up in front of a large audience if you want to educate people. I also learned early on that my ability to think on my feet and to make decisions quickly helped me in this career. A sense of humor and a touch of optimism are necessary for this job.

What schooling or training did you need to get this job?

Everything I learned in high school and college has helped me. To be an educator, you have to be educated. You have to have knowledge of your

field and you have to be able to transmit your knowledge to others.

Now I'm working on my master's degree in education to learn as much as possible about methods and techniques for successfully getting ideas across to the public.

What do you like most/least about your job?

I love working in a highly creative atmosphere. I enjoy working with my staff because we have a relationship of mutual respect. My staff may have problems, but they come up with solutions. We like it when children tell us that they have changed their attitudes or behavior toward animals because of the program.

I rarely get immediate feedback from the children. I can only hope that my efforts will result in a kinder and more informed attitude toward animals in the children who have attended these workshops.

What advice do you have for young people interested in humane education?

If you have the opportunity to set up environmental or animal-related clubs in grade school or high school, take the leadership role. Use the library to research topics of interest, such as ecology or animal behavior.

If you can, work with a veterinarian or at a shelter as a volunteer during your school breaks. Get involved in extracurricular activities that are related to writing or public speaking; work on science club projects; contact environmental groups for their literature.

What John Does at Work

John has to coordinate all programs, help in the preparation of all written and audiovisual materials for presentation, work closely with the humane educators, and be aware of the shelter's philosophy while doing all of this.

John also sees to it that his department runs smoothly, writes copy for newsletters, handles the departmental budget, and deals with any personnel problems. He also sets up special programs or workshops, and works with other humane education departments in developing new ideas and projects.

But with all the pressures and responsibilities, John is very happy with the job, his coworkers, and the goals of the shelter. He is also very happy when the animals are healthy and well cared for and find a loving home. That seems to make all the problems of the day disappear.

Let's Meet...

Karen Okura
Animal Behaviorist and Research Center Coordinator

Karen spends half of her day at the shelter developing a library and half of her day on the phone answering questions from owners who are having problems with their pets. She has been doing this for 2 years.

Tell me how you got started in humane work.

I started out 9 years ago as an adoption coordinator and kennel attendant. Then I was promoted to humane educator. I have been coordinator of the research center for 2 years. I got all my training here, at first as a volunteer working 16 hours a week.

Now I'm cataloging the collection, which is open on a limited basis. As soon as everything is organized, it will be opened as a lending library for the public. These books are also used as references to answer the calls I receive on the animal behavior hotline.

Describe a typical day at work.

I usually begin my workday with cataloging, filing, and sending out supplemental mailings for the hotline. I try to keep up on reviews of new publications and to place orders for new acquisitions.

What schooling or training did you need to get this job?

Before my training here, I had 2 years of college, where I had a lot of psychology courses. I never had any animal behavior or library courses, but I did serve as a peer counselor in high school. I think that studying about the human mind has helped me in working with owners on the hotline and, to a certain extent, in understanding animal behavior.

What do you like most/least about your job?

I like the Sherlock Holmes aspect of my job: I love figuring out solutions to problems, after I have researched them. I also love the positive feedback of owners who have taken my advice and solved the problem.

The least favorite part of the job for me is when an owner has no idea what the responsibilities of pet ownership are. This ignorance can lead to neglect and abuse of the animal and often the return of the animal to the shelter.

What advice do you have for young people interested in humane education?

Anyone interested in this aspect of humane education should definitely work with animals because they teach you about animal behavior better than anyone. You should also read as much as possible. Courses in biology, zoology, or animal behavior in high school or college would also be very helpful.

Karen's Changing Career

Karen remembers being exhilarated when she was hired as a full-time employee because she had enjoyed her work as a volunteer so much. Now she felt "official." But she was exhausted after the first 8-hour day with only a half hour for lunch. The work of an attendant is difficult physically, but it does build up your biceps.

Karen was used to working as part of a team when she was a humane educator in the schools. Now she works alone and has full responsibility for the resource center and hotline. Once in a while, though, she does get to work as a liaison with the education department because they both have the same goal: educating people about the needs of animals.

Karen is considering completing her college course work and getting her degree. In the meantime, Karen continues to educate herself through reading, attending lectures and seminars, and sharing information with other trainers.

Humane Society of the United States

The Humane Society of the United States was founded in 1954 to give a voice to animal concerns in this country. The underlying belief is that humans have an obligation to protect other species on this earth. The society works through legal, educational, legislative, and investigative channels. Pets, wild animals, laboratory animals, and farm animals are all under the watchful eye of this organization.

Ellen Sawyer

Ellen Sawyer, director of Tree House Animal Foundation, Inc., grew up with a compassion for all life, but she did not focus this feeling on animals until she met her cat Ruby. In fact, Ellen did not know very much about animals at all, but while she was sitting in the waiting room of her veterinarian with her sick little cat, she realized how much she had to learn and how much she wanted to help sick, injured, and neglected animals.

Luckily for her, in 1971 a group of innovative and creative people were trying to establish a cageless, no-kill adoption center. Ellen started out as a volunteer, worked part time as a veterinarian assistant, and eventually became director in 1983. She really learned about running an adoption center and taking care of cats during this period by devoting 24 hours a day to the endeavor. Today Tree House has become a model for shelters throughout the country.

Find Out More

You and humane work

Now that you have had a look at some educational possibilities in the humane field, it is time to take a look at yourself to see if you might be suited to this work. You will have to have a respect for animals and a kind feeling toward them. It is probably a good idea to work with animals and read as much about them as possible. If you have a pet of your own, learn about its habits, living conditions, and nutrition. Take full responsibility for its care. Educate yourself about animal behavior and needs; then try to educate your family and friends. Then you are really teaching, and that is what you would be doing as a humane educator.

The following questions are about other qualities, skills, and aptitudes you might have for this career.

1. Have you ever worked with your classmates on a project?

2. If you ever had to show anybody, such as your younger brother or sister or a classmate, how to do something (play baseball, tie a shoe, take care of a pet), did he or she understand you or did you have to repeat the instructions over and over again?

3. Do you like to write compositions, draw pictures, and read books?

4. Do you like to help your friends out when they are in trouble? Do you like to take care of people or animals when they are sick? Try to think of some examples when you have helped someone out.

5. Do you like to talk to people, either on the phone, in person, or maybe even from a stage? Have you ever been in a play at school? Did you enjoy it?

Find out more about humane work

The Humane Society of the United States
2100 L St. N.W.
Washington, DC 20037

Protecting the Web
The Anti-Cruelty Society of Chicago
157 W. Grand Ave.
Chicago, IL 60610

Mae Hickman and Maxine Guys,
Care of the Wild Feathered and Furred
New York:
Michael Kesend Publishing, Ltd., 1973

CAREERS
IN
AQUARIUMS

Aquariums, like zoos, need a wide variety of people to make them work. They need scientifically trained professionals to work directly with the animals, many others who support those professionals, and an administrative staff to make sure that everything works smoothly. Many modern aquariums have educational and research staffs, veterinarians, veterinary technicians, aquarists, and aquatic biologists.

If you have a goldfish or an aquarium at home, if you like to swim, dive, or snorkel, or if you really enjoy visiting the

aquarium or the ocean, you may be ready to think of a
career with an aquarium. We will learn about how you can
become an aquarist and then move up to being an assistant
curator. So let's dive in!

Let's find out what happens on the job

Aquarists are usually in charge of
a complete gallery. The first thing
in the morning they must make
the rounds. They check everything,
including water temperature,
cleanliness of tanks, health of
animals, and general conditions.
If there is a medical problem with
an animal, they will report it to the
veterinarian or the curator. When
all these details have been taken
care of, major feedings take place,
exhibits have to be prepared, and
tanks have to be designed and built.

Aquarists diagnose disease,
choose the proper antibiotics for the
sick animal, and set up quarantine
procedures. Animals, like humans,
can become ill from the environmental conditions and from stress.
A great deal of the aquarist's work
has to do with providing the correct
nutrition for each species and in
many cases that involves research.

Although the atmosphere may
be hectic and the hours long,
aquarists do get to go to meetings
and lectures throughout the United
States to exchange ideas with
others in the field. About once a
year, they go on collecting trips to
the Florida Keys, the Bahamas,

or Puerto Rico. On these collecting trips it is especially important to be able to work cooperatively as a member of the team. It also gives the aquarists a chance to show off their swimming, diving, and snorkeling skills!

The rewards, the pay, and the perks

Most people who work with animals of any kind, shape, or size will say that the work itself is the greatest reward, that each species enriches their lives in ways that cannot be measured in dollars and cents. They would continue their work the morning after they won the lottery.

For the privilege of working with the fishes of the world and for saving endangered species, you may have to be prepared to start out somewhere near $20,000 a year as an aquarist. As you move up to a middle management position, you may earn somewhere between $25,000 and $38,000 a year and as a top administrator, you will probably not earn more than $45,000.

Many aquariums offer tuition reimbursement programs for their employees. If you are really good at your job, there is also a good chance that you will be promoted. Most aquariums also have very good insurance, vacation, and holiday schedules.

Getting started

Many people begin to get interested in this work because they have tropical fish at home. In this way, you begin to realize the responsibilities you will have to maintain their health and well-being.

You may want to take swimming lessons and learn to dive, sail, or snorkel. Spend some time in your local aquarium, and if you are old enough to do some volunteer work there, it will teach you many things you could not learn anywhere else.

Your high school courses should include math, science—including biology—and English. If you can, start taking computer courses in high school, too.

Now decide if aquarium work is right for you

You might start out by asking yourself some questions:

- Am I willing to work long hours?
- Am I physically strong?
- Do I have what it takes to finish high school and go to college for 4 years?
- Do I like science courses, science fairs, and science activities?
- Do I like animals?
- Can I swim or am I afraid of the water?
- Do I care about endangered species and the environment?

- Am I responsible and dependable?

- Do I have keen observational
  skills?

- Can I work well alone and as
  part of a team?

If you can answer all of these
questions with "yes," you are well
on your way to a career in an
aquarium.

Let's Meet...

Steve Bezich
Aquarist

Steve is a senior aquarist in an aquarium in a major city. He has been there for 9 years. Working for and with these wonderful creatures is what he likes most.

Tell me how you got started in aquarium work.

I got started because of my love of water and fish and because I had carpentry and shop skills. My grandfather was a fisherman, my father was a crack carpenter, and my brother is a mechanic. I learned their skills and blended them to build a very rewarding career as an aquarist.

When I started out, it was not necessary to have a bachelor's degree to get an entry-level position as an aquarist, so my particular mix of skill and love made me a perfect volunteer at the aquarium. After 3 years as a volunteer, my special skills and acquired knowledge landed me the job of aquarist.

Describe a typical day at work.

There is no typical day, but there are typical things to do. The first thing to do every morning is to observe all the animals in the gallery. This means that all the fish

have to be checked, all the tanks have to be monitored, and the water level and pressure have to be controlled. Sick and injured animals take priority and will be attended to first. Big projects have to be planned for and strategized. If I am working with a volunteer, I have to give the volunteer instructions. I also have to report special problems to my curator.

What schooling or training did you need to get this job?

Now and in the future, all aquarists will have to have a degree from a 4-year college or university. Courses you should take in college should have an emphasis on the sciences, such as biology, marine biology, zoology, animal behavior, or animal husbandry. Self-educated aquarists like me will have a more difficult time in the future, and will probably only find any kind of opportunity in a small aquarium. My advice is to get as much formal education as possible.

What do you like most/least about your job?

The best part of the job is working with the animals. I also enjoy working with the other aquarists, not only at my aquarium, but also with those I meet at meetings. I like the diversity of my work and the independence and autonomy I have in performing my job.

I don't like the lack of a personal life, because this job demands long hours, weekend work, and covering for other aquarists when they are sick or on vacation. Even though I work for a large institution, I feel that it is understaffed and that the aquarists have to give up too much personal time.

Sending a Turtle Home

One of the most unforgettable experiences that Steve had
on the job was to release a 208-pound sea turtle back into its
natural habitat. One of the major functions of the modern
aquarium is to collect animals that are endangered and
breed them in captivity. When their number increases
enough, they are returned to the water.

To collect animals, the aquarists go out together on
annual collecting trips to the Bahamas. Several people have
to live together on a boat for approximately 2 weeks. That
kind of closeness requires a real sense of cooperation and
teamwork.

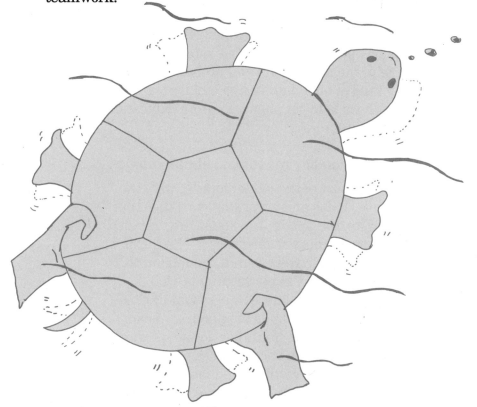

Let's Meet...

Jim Anderson
Assistant Curator of Fishes

Jim got interested in marine biology when he worked in Oregon, on the ocean. His job lets him work with fish and with people. That makes him very happy.

Tell me how you got started in aquarium management.

As an undergraduate, I majored in marine biology. I went on to get my master's degree in fisheries with an emphasis on fish diseases. I worked as a public education coordinator for a marine science center and as an aquarist before being promoted to assistant curator.

Describe a typical day at work.

I spend about 50 percent of my day in administration and 50 percent in husbandry (the science of animal production). The first thing in the morning I have to monitor the entire aquarium. I have to have a feel for all the collections, know the problem areas, check on the sick or injured animals, be accessible to the aquarists, and make sure that all tanks are clean.

In the afternoon, I have to deal with personnel problems, sched-ules, and evaluations, and order supplies. Since I am a specialist in

fish diseases, I may also spend some time in
the laboratory in order to help with diagnoses.

What schooling or training did you need to get this job?

It is essential to have a degree from a 4-year
college or university to get into aquarium
management now. It is a good idea to get a
broad-based educational background with
emphasis on the natural sciences. In addition,
you should study math, all phases of English,
including oral and writing skills, and computer skills. Since much of environmental
work is global, knowledge of a foreign lan-
guage may also be helpful. Because of the
administrative skills needed for my job, I also
recently received my master's of business
administration from night school.

What do you like most/least about your job?

My favorite thing about the job is working
with the fish. I also like organizing and lead-
ing collecting trips to the Florida Keys or the
Bahamas. During these trips, a group of
aquarists will collect species that are needed
for the aquarium's collection or that are con-
sidered endangered.

The least favorite thing is seeing an animal
die, especially one you have become attached
to or devoted extra effort to. The inevitable
crises contribute to stress because all else has
to stop while the problem is being solved.
My salary is not what I like the most about
the job.

Jim Learns From the Fish

Jim has some very clear ideas about what it takes to be successful in aquarium management. He follows the maxim that the animal is always right. If he follows that, everything else falls into place. He will also say that you should "believe" the animal. If the expert says the animal should behave in one way, and the animal behaves in another way, the animal is right.

You have to understand the fish. This comes with everyday contact as well as through classroom study. Jim never stops learning in his job.

Success Stories

Tennessee Aquarium

The Tennessee Aquarium in Chatta-
nooga boasts of being the first major
freshwater life center in the world.
Exhibits range from the Tennessee
River and the Mississippi Delta to
the great rivers of Africa, South America, Siberia, and Asia.
Natural habitats of fish, birds, amphibians, reptiles, mammals, and insects are recreated in 21 exhibits with more
than 7,000 examples of 350 species. All of this is housed in a
12-story building that holds 400,000 gallons of water. The
aquarium also houses the largest freshwater tank in the
world—138,000 gallons!

More than 150,000 schoolchildren visit the aquarium on
field trips. They may see a puppet show, a documentary, or
video programs on freshwater habitats. A 200-seat audito-
rium and classrooms are also available for educational
purposes. You will also see the 60-foot-high central canyon
with ramps and bridges that connect five levels; you feel
that you are in the water. There is a lot to see and learn in
this very special aquarium.

Find Out More

You and aquarium work

Now it is time for you to think seriously about yourself in aquarium work. Let's see how you might be able to decide whether you are suited to it.

First, let's review the skills and qualities you will need to be successful as an aquarist or aquarium manager:

1. You will have to have a college degree.

2. You have to like working with animals.

3. You have to have good grades in science, math, and English.

4. You will have to know how to operate a computer.

5. You have to be dependable and responsible.

6. You have to be patient, have a good sense of humor, and be able to work as a team member.

7. You have to be able to solve problems and make quick decisions.

8. You should be a good swimmer and diver.

9. You should be able to live on a tight budget.

10. You should be able to understand people as well as fish.

Since you already know about the educational requirements for aquarium work, you might want to take a look at your study habits and your actual grades in grade school and high school. If they need improvement, now is the time to do something about it.

If you have no pets now, it may be a good idea to start out with some goldfish or a small aquarium of tropical fish. It this is not possible, you could perhaps arrange with neighbors to help them take care of their animals, especially when they are at work or on vacation. As soon as you are old enough to volunteer at the local zoo or aquarium, you should. Take swimming lessons at school or on your summer vacation. Get experience on an actual boat if you can.

Now see how you might answer these questions:

1. Do you see yourself in a glamorous job making a lot of money?

2. Do you need someone to remind you to do your chores?

3. Do you like to play games with other people?

4. Are you able to make judgments on your own?

5. Do you like physical exercise?

You would probably be a good aquarium worker if your answers are: 1–no, 2–no, 3–yes, 4–yes, 5–yes.

CAREERS IN TRAINING

I f you are thinking about becoming a trainer of animals, you are in luck. There are trainers for just about any type of animal. Animals are trained for different reasons and trainers are needed all over the country.

If you think you might like to become a trainer, you just have to decide which kind of animal you would like to work with. Then you will have to decide whether you would like to work as a neighborhood obedience trainer, with exotic animals for the movies, with guide dogs, or with the government. Whichever choice you make, there are many opportunities open to you.

What it's like to be a trainer

Although your training techniques will vary according to the animal and the purpose of the training, some things will be the same for all trainers. Most trainers will agree that you have to be physically strong and mentally aware, since you will be working so closely with the animals. You should have a thorough understanding of the way those animals behave and react. You also should have an understanding of the particular animal you are working with. You must love to work with animals!

Let's find out what happens on the job

There is probably no typical day that would apply to every trainer because of the differences in the animals and the purpose of the training. A trainer may work with just one animal at a time or an entire kennel or stable on any given day. Trainers may also be responsible for the care and feeding of the animals they are training. That means bathing and grooming them, walking them, playing with them, even preparing their food and feeding them. Some trainers also give classes or counseling sessions to the owners so that they will be able to keep up the good work of the trainer when the animal returns home. Trainers may be self-employed or work for large training centers or farms. Some work part time, while others are full-time trainers of very specific skills for very specific animals. The field is wide open to you as a trainer.

The pleasures and pressures of the job

Trainers are like other people who work with animals because they say the biggest pleasure of the job is working with the animals. Depending on the purpose of the training, the other pleasures may vary. For example, if you were an obedience trainer for dogs, the pleasure would come again when the dog obeys commands and behaves well— and the owner is happy with the "new" dog.

If you trained animals for movies or television shows, your pleasure would come when the animal responded to the directions in the script and people were entertained. If you trained animals to assist the handicapped, the fact that a blind or deaf person finds a new independence because of your training would be the next best pleasure besides the actual training.

Pressures surrounding the trainer's job would be related to the possibility of injury to the animals in your care. Sometimes owners expect too much too soon from their animals and do not understand that training is a process that is ongoing, not something that just happens overnight.

The rewards, the pay, and the perks

The best reward of the job for a trainer is being with animals. The pay and perks will vary according to a few factors: whether you are self employed; whether you work full time; whether you work for a large training center or farm; and whether you perform other services, such as selling pet products or providing pet-sitting services.

If you are self employed, you will be able to set your own fees and services. It may be a little risky financially until you get customers. But after that, you can make a good living as a trainer. You will, however, also be responsible for your own insurance and retirement plans for yourself and your employees. If you work for someone else, including state and federal agencies, you will receive standard pay ranges and benefits.

Getting started

If you are thinking about becoming a trainer, you should get as much experience with animals as possible. If you have a dog, try now to see whether it responds to you, whether you have an easy way with it, and whether you feel a sense of responsibility toward it.

If you live in a rural area, spend time with horses at a local farm. If you live near a racetrack, see if it needs volunteers and work with the horses during your summer breaks.

Many trainers have college degrees in animal behavior, biology, animal science, or veterinary technology. Others have trained under other top trainers in their field. Government agencies usually have strict requirements that you may want to check into.

Things you can do to get a head start

If you think you have any natural abilities in training animals, you may want to start refining them by working with animals in your neighborhood, as well as your own pet. Visit farms and zoos to learn more about large animals and exotic animals and birds. Read about animal behavior and needs. Go to movies about animals and watch special shows on television about animals. You can even rent videos about animal training. When you are old enough, get into a volunteer program at the zoo or with a veterinarian. Research the top trainers in your area and apply to them during the summer. This is a very good way to work into a full-time job and an eventual career.

Let's Meet...

Jim Morgan
Obedience Trainer

Jim is convinced that he is part dog because he is so happy when he is with them. He has been a trainer as long as he can remember and would not change a minute of it.

Tell me how you got started in obedience training.

Several years ago, I was training my own dog. Someone pulled up in a car and said he would pay me to train his dog. I had always worked with dogs for fun, but I never thought anyone could make a living training them. For many years, I did not have a building I could call a workplace, so I worked from my car. I would load it up with assorted dogs and take them to the park to train them. I built up a business with this method and am delighted it all worked out so well.

Describe a typical day at work.

I start my day at 4:30 A.M. when I feed and walk the dogs. Then I take some time out to work out, usually until about 8 A.M. Then I train the dogs until about noon. From noon to about 2 P.M. is rest period and then training goes on from 2 to 6 P.M. My family and I live in the same house as the kennels, so I am always with the dogs. It does not leave any real time for vacations or time off. I have a full-time staff of four and six volunteers I am training. I give clients training courses so they can volunteer there too. I also give follow-up training sessions to owners who want to learn the process when their dogs get home.

What schooling or training did you need to get this job?

When I started out, I had no formal training. Since then, though, I have attended many seminars led by the top trainers in the field. I believe I have read every book that has ever been printed about dog training, but you learn far more from working with the animals than you will learn from books. Dogs are predictable, but different. Each needs something different, but no dog needs force. Flexibility in handling the dogs is a necessary aspect of being a good trainer.

What advice do you have for young people interested in obedience training?

Go to as many obedience training classes in the local park system as possible. Watch and listen. Be patient and be positive and work with as many dogs as possible. Remember that anger teaches nothing, and that your voice is for praise; it is not a weapon. Try to volunteer with the best people. They are usually very cooperative in sharing their knowledge. Let them know that you want to do it right. If you love it, you should pursue it. But you should be prepared for long hours, strenuous physical work, and a great amount of satisfaction.

Jim's Best Friends

Jim is physically and spiritually connected to dogs. The connection is deep and strong—after all, he is "part dog." He needs to have dogs in his life, especially when things go wrong.

Once he hit a roller skater with his car. As it turned out, the person he hit was all right, but Jim was scared. He saw to it that the victim was taken care of, and then he went home, still shaken. The first thing he did was to open all the kennels and let all the dogs out. They gave him the love and reassurance he needed. Dogs have no moods, they make no judgments, and they are always there.

Again, after his father died, he sought comfort from his dog Harry. They drove around for hours and even though Jim was very tired, he needed that time with his best friend, his dog.

Let's Meet...

Karl Mikolka
Trainer of Dressage Horses

Karl is a world-famous expert in training the renowned Lipizzan horses. He also judges dressage, a special kind of precision training for horses.

Tell me how you got started in dressage training.

I come from Vienna, Austria, and I was always interested in horses. When I was young, horses were still used as transportation, so I saw them a lot. My mother told me that I used to jump up and down making clicking sounds whenever I saw a horse—and I was still in a stroller. I spent time as a teen-ager hanging around horse stables; then I became a groom at a racetrack, where I was allowed to exercise the trotters. Eventually I applied to the Spanish Riding School and the rest is history.

Describe a typical day at work.

I start training horses at about 7:30 in the morning. I also give lessons to private students at this time. Afternoons are spent giving mini-clinics and weekends may include 2- or 3-day clinics here in the United States or as far away as Australia or Japan.

What schooling or training did you need to get this job?

I spent 14 years at the Spanish Riding School in Vienna. I think that is more than adequate training for any position anywhere in the training of dressage horses and riders. I have also served as coach of the Brazilian dressage team. This training has held me in good stead for the 30 years I have spent with these splendid white stallions.

What do you like most/least about your job?

I love working with horses and having the opportunity to be a part of nature in a very special way. What I do not like is a lame horse or a horse that dies. Some physical hardships are also involved in this job, as well as owners who can be difficult.

What advice do you have for young people interested in dressage training?

I recommend a good general education for anyone who wants to train. You might even think about being able to support yourself in an unrelated field, because it is hard to become financially successful in this field. I recommend getting a sponsor if you can, because your love of the horse is the most important thing for a trainer. You can only hope that you can make a good living from it.

What do you see yourself doing 5 years from now?

I can only hope to win the lottery so I can buy two Lipizzans for myself—just for the fun of it!

Some Precision Moves of the Lipizzans

Dressage training means that the horse performs precision movements at the trainer's command. Precision movements for a Lipizzan are comparable to those of a dancer. They do remarkable things, thanks in great part to their "choreographer," the trainer.

The *piaffe* is much like running in place.

The horse stands on its hind legs in a *levade.*

In the *ballotade,* the horse jumps into the air with its body horizontal. The *capriole* is similar, except the horse's hind legs are stretched out. This was originally meant to keep enemies away.

If a horse leaps on its hind legs several times, it is doing a *courbette.*

Success Stories

Carolyn Resnick

Carolyn Resnick is a horse trainer with a personal touch. She has developed a seven-step program that helps the trainer understand how horses act with one another. Her program is called Dancing with Horses. Understanding how horses interact helps her to become friends with horses.

Horses have a strong sense of community that respects the individual horse and how it relates to the herd. If you see the movie *Black Stallion*, you will see the same kind of relationship between the horse and the boy that Carolyn tries to create in her training sessions.

The Tempel Lipizzans

If you have never seen these magnificent horses going through their routines, you are in for a pleasant surprise. This extraordinary breed originated in Austria more than 400 years ago and the horses have been performing in the Spanish Riding School in Vienna since then. Walt Disney even made a movie about them called *The Miracle of the White Stallions*.

These are strong horses, capable of jumping from the ground with all four feet and then forcefully kicking out with their hind feet. These graceful horses perform balletlike movements with ease. There are only about 2,000 pure Lipizzans in the world today and about 5 percent are now in the United States.

Find Out More

You and training

Now that you have read about what it takes to be a trainer, you can begin to determine whether this is the life for you. You will have a variety of choices if you decide to train, so you will want to think about which type of animal you would like to train and what you would like to train it for. Let's begin.

1. Imagine yourself training an animal. Which animal do you see yourself with? A horse, a dog, or a wild animal?

2. Now that you have decided about the animal, what are you training it for? Obedience, entertainment, guide, protection, law enforcement?

3. Now imagine where you might like to work. Would you like to be self-employed, in a large training center, with the government, on a farm, in a movie studio, or in a circus?

4. Do you think you are patient? Sensitive? Capable of leadership? Ready to work hard? Willing to learn?

5. Are you willing to do volunteer work? Read and learn about animals? Work long hours? Be responsible?

6. Can you think of five reasons you would like to be a trainer?

If you can see yourself as a trainer, you can be one. You just have to have the dream and then make it happen.

Now decide if veterinary work is right for you

"Animal Trainers," Occupational Brief 508
Chronicle Guidance Publications
Aurora Street Extension
P.O. Box 1190
Moravia, NY 13118-1190

The American Equine Association
Box 658
Newfoundland, NJ 07435

Guide Dogs for the Blind
611 Granite Springs Road
Yorktown Heights, NY 10598

CAREERS

IN

WILDLIFE

Both the federal and state governments offer careers in wildlife management and conservation of natural resources. One of the major federal employers is the U.S. Fish and Wildlife Service of the Department of the Interior. It hires wildlife biologists, research biologists, fishery biologists, and refuge managers. Since the federal government has strict educational requirements for all job offerings, you should find out what they are before planning your future career.

Every state has a conservation or natural resources department, usually in the state capital. Their jobs are similar to those in the federal government, and their educational standards may be just as strict. Now is the time to contact them to see if there are any volunteer programs available.

What it's like to be in wildlife work

You will, of course, have to have a deep commitment to the environment in general, conservation and preservation of species in particular, and a feeling for how we all can live together harmoniously if you want to work with wildlife. You may be working outdoors directly with the animals, fish, and plants. Or you may work primarily in an office as an administrator or educator.

Let's find out what happens on the job

If you are a wildlife biologist, you might plan wildlife programs, be involved in research projects, help to recreate wildlife habitats, and try to prevent disease. Research biologists study whole populations of wild animals and their relationship with other animals and plant life. They may also be involved with taking a census count of the animals and researching nutritional needs. Fishery biologists are concerned with classification, rearing, and stocking fisheries. Wildlife areas also need managers who oversee wildlife and fish and agents who enforce laws and regulations. Various technicians constitute the support staff for the biologists. Educating the public about wildlife is now becoming a major part of many wildlife agencies, so you can become a wildlife interpreter or education specialist.

The pleasures and pressures of the job

As a biologist, you get to work directly with the animals outdoors in their natural environment and in good weather, that is a pleasure. Preserving the various species and conserving their habitats is a special pleasure.

Meeting the goals of the agency you work for when the budget is tight or when the staff is not very big can pose particular problems. And dealing with injured animals or trying to save endangered species can also be difficult.

Getting started

Although state and federal agencies are the major employers for people in wildlife, private parks or refuges are also possibilities for careers.

Check education and training requirements with these various agencies before you start high school. That way, you can plan your course work with your specific career in mind.

Volunteer at your local zoo, wildlife park, or refuge.

Read as much as you can about wildlife, habitats, natural environments, and ecological systems; watch television programs about wildlife.

Take your science courses and clubs seriously. Work on projects that will help you learn more about nature. Join local environmental groups or clubs and do volunteer work there.

Now decide if wildlife biology is right for you

If you have a curiosity about natural life—animals, plants, or fish—you may be on the way to a career in wildlife. Getting good grades in subjects that have to do with the natural environment, such as biology, zoology, or husbandry, is an important step.

1. If you had a choice between watching cartoons on television or walking in the woods, which would you do? Why?

2. Are you able to change your plans if an emergency comes up? How do you react to change?

3. Can you stick to a project and get it done, or do you tend to quit if it gets difficult?

If you prefer walking in the woods to watching cartoons, you are probably someone who is interested in nature and who would probably be happy working with wildlife. If you are flexible and can change plans, you have another positive quality for wildlife work. Being able to complete jobs that you have begun is also essential for conservation and preservation work.

Let's Meet...

Mamie Parker
Fish and Wildlife Biologist

Mamie is division chief for habitat conservation for the U.S. Fish and Wildlife Service. She has overcome many obstacles to be the success she is today.

Tell me how you got started in wildlife biology.

I grew up in Arkansas and spent a lot of time fishing. The bass I caught in the morning I usually ate for lunch. Afternoons were spent asking other people who were fishing all about the various fish. In school, I was very good in biology and also began collecting things and examining their habitats (the types of places in which plants and animals live). When I was at the University of Arkansas, I met a recruiter from the U.S. Fish and Wildlife Service who was very impressed with me. The recruiter was looking specifically for members of minority groups and convinced my mother that the service would take good care of me. I was on my way to a 6-month internship and eventually a full-time job at a hatchery.

What schooling or training did you need to get this job?

I got my bachelor's degree at the University of Arkansas and went on to get my master's degree and doctorate. Then I worked for 10 years in Missouri, where I reviewed construction projects and how they would affect fish and wildlife habitats. A little more than a year ago, I became division chief, a management position. I was ready for this promotion because of my extensive education and experience.

What do you like most/least about your job?

I love to meet new people and to travel to fun places, and I get to do this in my job. These are two favorite pleasures. I also feel I am making a major contribution by saving animals' homes.

However, since I am a Southerner working in a northern state and a black person working in a predominantly white environment, I am lonely sometimes—and a little homesick. The workforce is also mostly male.

What advice do you have for young people interested in wildlife?

Take all the math and science courses you can. Do volunteer work at zoos or wildlife refuges as soon as you are old enough. Find a mentor who may guide you along your career path. This should be someone in the field with whom you could communicate in person or in writing. You could also go to day camps where you can get a feel for the outdoors by renting a boat or going fishing.

Mamie's Typical Day

Mamie has long days, but they are filled with opportunities to walk in the woods to observe wildlife.

She also gets to go scuba diving in the rivers and lakes to take count of the fish.

Mamie also studies biological information related to endangered species and talks to farmers, city leaders, and government officials to share ideas on protecting wildlife habitats.

Let's Meet...

Kathleen Andrews
Education Chief

Kathleen has successfully combined her love of the outdoors, knowledge of biology, and ability to educate into a career in a state conservation agency.

Tell me how you got started in conservation education.

My father was a college biology teacher and my family always spent time outdoors, picnicking, birding, fishing, hiking, or simply taking country drives. I also attended Girl Scout camps and was a camp counselor when I was in college. I received my bachelor's and master's degrees in wildlife biology and participated in agency programs involved with education.

Describe a typical day at work.

There is no typical day, but I can describe typical responsibilities. For example, I could be sitting at my computer writing articles. I also have to attend meetings to review and edit materials. I organize outdoor teaching opportunities and lead youth activities. I also make presentations to promote the use of environmental educational materials and raise money for the production of future materials.

What schooling or training did you need to get this job?

You will need at least a B.S., preferably in zoology or biology, and probably even an M.S. You will also need to know basic principles of ecology in order to convey your ideas through educational materials. An education degree would also be helpful as well as a love of the outdoors.

What do you like most/least about your job?

I like the freedom I have to create new and exciting materials that may reach someone who would otherwise not be environmentally aware. The difficult part of the job has to do with the statewide nature of it. I have to provide materials for teachers and devise programs to be used throughout the entire state. I also do not have as much direct contact with children as I would like.

What do you see yourself doing 5 years from now?

I intend to remain in the natural resources field and hope to have some connection with education. I have enjoyed a variety of positions since I graduated from college and would still select this as a career because I get a great deal of satisfaction from it.

Kathleen's Advice for Students

1. Plan your schooling to provide a solid foundation in the natural sciences or education.

2. Take courses in biology, botany, and education.

3. Specialized classes, such as ornithology, mammalogy, herpetology, journalism, and outdoor recreation will strengthen your knowledge and base skills.

4. Develop other skills that will give you the advantage over other job applicants, such as computer, public speaking, or grant-writing skills.

5. Look for opportunities to attend conferences, workshops, and training seminars related to wildlife.

Jane
Goodall
One of the most famous women to work with wild animals in Africa is Jane Goodall. For more than 30 years, she has worked with, documented, and been a friend to the chimpanzees at Gombe. She was a graduate of a secretarial school when she first went to Tanzania in 1960 to begin a lifelong relationship with these animals. Since then, she has earned a Ph.D. at Cambridge and has written books about her experiences: *In the Shadow of Man, Through a Window,* and *The Chimpanzees of Gombe: Patterns of Behavior.*

The
Sierra Club
The Sierra Club was founded in 1892 and has been active in working for environmental causes and endangered species since then. It has supported efforts to enlarge national park sites and has opposed the building of dams in many of these parks. The club has 100,000 members in all states and countries whose purpose is to work with legislators and other environmental groups to preserve wildlife refuges, endangered species, and natural resources.

Find Out More

You and wildlife

Now it is time for you to make some decisions about you and a career in wildlife. You can begin by answering the following questions:

1. Are you curious about the world around you? If so, give an example in your life.

2. Do you like to go to the zoo or take long walks in the woods or in the park? If so, how many times in the last year did you do any of those activities?

3. When you watch TV shows or read books, are they usually about nature or animals? Name some of the shows you like the best or books you have read in the past year.

4. Are you able to explain directions or instructions to other people? If so, write down at least one example of your teaching something to someone else.

5. Do you like to meet new people or are you very shy? Give some examples of how you feel about meeting new people.

If you were able to answer positively to these five questions, you have the

makings of someone who might be
very happy with a carer in wildlife.

If you have not taken a walk in
the woods or in a local park lately, it
is definitely time to get involved at
this level. As you walk, be obser-
vant. Look at the trees and plants,
and watch for any animals that
might be there. Ask the rangers
questions about their habits and
habitats, their needs and nutrition.
Then follow up in the library. Take
out every book you can about the
environment. Watch television
programs about wildlife, animals,
plants, fish—anything that will give
you an idea about your future
career. Then volunteer for a nature
group in your area.

INDEX

85